D0513544

MOURIN
THE SPECIAL

MOURINHO
THE SPECIAL ONE

THE LEGENDARY MANAGER
IN HIS OWN WORDS

EBURY
PRESS

3 5 7 9 10 8 6 4 2

Published in 2013 by Ebury Press, an imprint of Ebury Publishing
A Random House Group company

Copyright © Ebury Press

This book is not affiliated with, authorised or endorsed by José Mourinho

The Random House Group Limited Reg. No. 954009

Addresses for companies within the Random House Group
can be found at www.randomhouse.co.uk

A CIP catalogue record for this book is available from the British Library

Penguin Random House is committed to a sustainable future for
our business, our readers and our planet. This book is made from
Forest Stewardship Council® certified paper.

Printed and bound in Great Britain by Clays Ltd, St Ives plc

ISBN 9780091959807

To buy books by your favourite authors and register for offers visit
www.randomhouse.co.uk

INTRODUCING...

'HELLO, MISTER.
I'M JOSÉ MOURINHO'

Greeting new Sporting Lisbon manager
Bobby Robson on his arrival at Lisbon airport.
Mourinho would go on to act as Robson's
translator and assistant at Lisbon
and Barcelona, 1992

'EL TRADUCTOR'

*Mourinho's nickname at Barcelona
(the translator)*

'DON'T DOUBT THAT SOONER OR LATER I WILL GO TO A BIGGER CLUB'

Opening speech to his Uniao de Lieria players,
on becoming manager in 2001

'I'M SURE THAT PORTO WILL BE CHAMPIONS AT THE END OF MY FIRST FULL SEASON'

On joining Porto a year later, 2002

'PLEASE DON'T CALL ME ARROGANT BUT I AM EUROPEAN CHAMPION AND I THINK I'M A SPECIAL ONE'

On becoming Chelsea manager, 2004

'THE EGO HAS LANDED'

Sun headline after the 'Special One'
press conference, 2004

'I HAVE ARRIVED AT A SPECIAL CLUB AND I BELIEVE I AM A GREAT COACH BUT I DON'T WANT TO BE SPECIAL. I AM MOURINHO – THAT'S ALL'

On becoming manager at Inter, 2008

'I AM JOSÉ MOURINHO AND I DON'T CHANGE. I ARRIVE WITH ALL MY QUALITIES AND ALL MY DEFECTS'

On becoming Real Madrid head coach, 2010

'LIKE ME OR NOT, I AM THE ONLY ONE WHO HAS WON THE WORLD'S THREE MOST IMPORTANT LEAGUES. SO MAYBE INSTEAD OF THE "SPECIAL ONE", PEOPLE SHOULD START CALLING ME THE "ONLY ONE"'

On his success in guiding Real Madrid to the Spanish title, 2012

'I AM THE HAPPY ONE'

On his return to Chelsea, 2013

JOSÉ
METAPHOR-INHO

'IT'S LIKE HAVING A BLANKET THAT IS TOO SMALL FOR THE BED. YOU PULL THE BLANKET UP TO KEEP YOUR CHEST WARM AND YOUR FEET STICK OUT. I CANNOT BUY A BIGGER BLANKET BECAUSE THE SUPERMARKET IS CLOSED. BUT THE BLANKET IS MADE OF CASHMERE'

Injury crisis during first spell at Chelsea, 2007

'A LITTLE HORSE THAT STILL NEEDS MILK AND TO LEARN HOW TO JUMP. A HORSE THAT NEXT SEASON CAN RACE'

*On Chelsea's title chances, after beating
Manchester City 1-0, 2014*

'NO EGGS, NO OMELETTES. AND IT DEPENDS ON THE QUALITY OF THE EGGS'

On Roman Abramovich's comments that he wants Chelsea to win with style, 2007

'IN THE SUPERMARKET, YOU HAVE CLASS ONE, CLASS TWO, CLASS THREE. SOME ARE MORE EXPENSIVE THAN OTHERS AND SOME GIVE YOU BETTER OMELETTES. SO WHEN THE CLASS ONE EGGS ARE IN WAITROSE AND YOU CANNOT GO THERE YOU HAVE A PROBLEM'

Elaborating on his egg metaphor.
No, still none the wiser!

'THE MORAL OF THE STORY IS NOT TO LISTEN TO THOSE WHO TELL YOU NOT TO PLAY THE VIOLIN BUT STICK TO THE TAMBOURINE'

On winning the Premier League, 2005

'WHY DRIVE AN ASTON MARTIN ALL THE TIME, WHEN I HAVE A FERRARI AND PORSCHE AS WELL? THAT WOULD JUST BE STUPID'

On selecting Joe Cole, Damien Duff and Arjen Robben for different matches, 2005

'YOUNG PLAYERS ARE A
LITTLE BIT LIKE MELONS...
SOMETIMES YOU HAVE
BEAUTIFUL MELONS, BUT
THEY DON'T TASTE VERY
GOOD AND SOME OTHER
MELONS ARE A BIT UGLY
AND WHEN YOU OPEN
THEM THE TASTE
IS FANTASTIC'

*Expanding on Chelsea's youth policy
(we think), 2007*

'IF YOU HAVE A FERRARI AND I HAVE SOME SMALL CAR, I HAVE TO PUNCTURE YOUR TYRES OR PUT SUGAR IN YOUR PETROL TANK'

Explaining (sort of) his tactics against Barcelona, 2010

'THE BIGGER THE SHIP, THE STRONGER THE STORM. FORTUNATELY FOR ME, I HAVE ALWAYS BEEN IN BIG SHIPS... NOW I'M AT REAL MADRID, WHICH IS CONSIDERED THE BIGGEST SHIP ON THE PLANET'

On his appointment at Real Madrid, 2010

'I LOOK FORWARD TO THE SALT AND PEPPER OF FOOTBALL'

On returning to the Premier League, 2013

'A GREAT PIANIST DOESN'T RUN AROUND THE PIANO OR DO PUSH-UPS WITH THE TIPS OF HIS FINGERS. TO BE GREAT HE PLAYS THE PIANO... BEING A GREAT FOOTBALLER IS NOT ABOUT RUNNING, PUSH-UPS OR PHYSICAL WORK GENERALLY. THE BEST WAY TO BE A GREAT FOOTBALLER IS TO PLAY FOOTBALL'

On being a great footballer, 2005

'BEAUTIFUL YOUNG EGGS. EGGS THAT NEED A MUM OR, IN THIS CASE, A DAD TO TAKE CARE OF THEM, TO KEEP THEM WARM DURING THE WINTER, TO BRING THE BLANKET AND IMPROVE THEM'

Swapping eggs for melons in talking about Chelsea's young players, 2013

'SOMETIMES YOU SEE BEAUTIFUL PEOPLE WITH NO BRAINS. SOMETIMES YOU HAVE UGLY PEOPLE WHO ARE INTELLIGENT, LIKE SCIENTISTS. OUR PITCH IS A BIT LIKE THAT. FROM THE TOP IT'S A DISGRACE BUT THE BALL ROLLS AT A NORMAL SPEED'

On the state of the Stamford Bridge pitch, 2006

JOSÉ VERSUS THE PREMIER LEAGUE

'THEY BROUGHT THE BUS AND LEFT THE BUS IN FRONT OF GOAL'

On Tottenham's defensive tactics after a
0-0 draw at Stamford Bridge, 2004

'THIS IS FOOTBALL FROM THE 19TH CENTURY'

*On being held to a goalless draw by
Sam Allardyce's West Ham, 2014*

'THE ONLY THING I CAN BRING MORE TO WIN WAS A BLACK AND DECKER'

Mixing the metaphors over West Ham's tactics

'HE CAN'T TAKE IT BECAUSE WE'VE OUTWITTED HIM... HE CAN TELL ME ALL HE WANTS, I DON'T GIVE A SHIT'

Sam Allardyce responds to Mourinho's criticisms

'I WANT TO GIVE MY CONGRATULATIONS TO THEM BECAUSE THEY WON. BUT WE WERE THE BEST TEAM. WE DIDN'T LOSE THE GAME'

*On Chelsea losing on penalties to Charlton
in the Carling Cup, 2005*

'IN TRAINING, I OFTEN
PLAY MATCHES OF
THREE AGAINST THREE
AND WHEN THE SCORE
REACHES 5-4 I SEND
THE PLAYERS BACK TO
THE DRESSING ROOM
BECAUSE THEY ARE NOT
DEFENDING PROPERLY'

On Arsenal's 5-4 victory over Tottenham, 2004

**'ROBBIE SAVAGE
COMMITS 20 FOULS
DURING THE GAME AND
NEVER GETS A BOOKING.
WE CAME HERE TO PLAY
FOOTBALL AND IT WAS
NOT A FOOTBALL GAME,
IT WAS A FIGHT'**

*On Blackburn's physical approach
against Chelsea, 2005*

'WE ARE ON TOP AT
THE MOMENT BUT NOT
BECAUSE OF THE CLUB'S
FINANCIAL POWER. WE
ARE IN CONTENTION
FOR A LOT OF TROPHIES
BECAUSE OF MY
HARD WORK'

*On the reasons behind Chelsea
leading the title race, 2005*

'IN ENGLAND, WHICH CLUB PLAYS BETTER THAN CHELSEA? ARSENAL? 10 POINTS BEHIND'

On criticism of how Chelsea play, 2005

'A PLAYER FROM MAN CITY SHOWED HALF OF HIS ASS FOR TWO SECONDS AND IT WAS A BIG NIGHTMARE. BUT THIS IS A REAL NIGHTMARE'

On the head injuries Petr Cech suffered in the Chelsea match again Reading, in comparison to the furore over Joey Barton baring all, 2006

'ONE DAY SOMEBODY WILL PUNCH YOU'

*Friendly advice for a Crystal Palace ball boy,
who wouldn't give the ball back, 2014*

JOSÉ VERSUS BARCELONA

'TODAY, TOMORROW, ALWAYS WITH BARCELONA IN MY HEART'

*Declaring his love for Barcelona after
they won the Copa del Ray in 1997*

'MY HISTORY AS A MANAGER CANNOT BE COMPARED WITH FRANK RIJKAARD'S HISTORY. HE HAS ZERO TROPHIES AND I HAVE A LOT OF THEM'

On the then Barcelona coach before a Barcelona-Chelsea Champions League match, 2005

'WHEN I SAW RIJKAARD ENTERING THE REFEREE'S DRESSING ROOM I COULDN'T BELIEVE IT. WHEN DIDIER DROGBA WAS SENT OFF I WASN'T SURPRISED'

Making claims about half-time shenanigans during the Barcelona-Chelsea Champions League clash, 2005

'IF I TELL UEFA WHAT I
REALLY THINK AND FEEL,
MY CAREER WOULD
END NOW. INSTEAD
I WILL JUST ASK A
QUESTION TO WHICH I
HOPE ONE DAY TO GET
A RESPONSE: WHY?'

*Mourinho accuses UEFA of a pro-Barcelona
bias which makes it impossible for his
team to win, 2011*

'WHY OVREBRO? WHY BUSACCA? WHY DE BLEECKERE? WHY STARK... WHY DOES A TEAM AS GOOD AS THEY ARE NEED SOMETHING [EXTRA] THAT IS SO OBVIOUS THAT EVERYONE SEES IT?'

*On the various referees Mourinho claims have
helped Barcelona over the years, 2011*

'TOMORROW WE WILL PROBABLY READ I AM TO BLAME FOR THE VOLCANO. MAYBE I HAVE A FRIEND IN THE VOLCANO AND I AM RESPONSIBLE FOR THAT'

On Barcelona's suggestion that the Eyjafjallajökull volcano hampered their preparations for the Champions League match against Inter, 2010

'WE DID NOT PARK THE BUS, WE PARKED THE PLANE'

On Inter losing against Barcelona in the Champions League semi-final second leg, but going through on aggregate, 2010

JOSÉ
VERSUS PEP

'HERE [THE REAL MADRID PRESS ROOM], HE IS THE CHIEF, THE FUCKING MAN. IN HERE HE IS THE FUCKING MAN AND I CAN'T COMPETE WITH HIM'

Pep Guardiola on Mourinho and his mind games, before the 2011 Champions League semi-final between Real Madrid and Barcelona

'ONE DAY I WOULD LIKE JOSEP GUARDIOLA TO WIN THIS COMPETITION PROPERLY'

*After Real Madrid's controversial 2-0 defeat
to Barcelona in the Champions League
semi-final first leg, 2011*

'JOSEP GUARDIOLA IS
A FANTASTIC COACH,
BUT I HAVE WON TWO
CHAMPIONS LEAGUES. HE
HAS WON ONE CHAMPIONS
LEAGUE AND THAT IS ONE
THAT WOULD EMBARRASS
ME. I WOULD BE ASHAMED
TO HAVE WON IT WITH
THE SCANDAL OF
STAMFORD BRIDGE'

Mourinho not letting the matter rest, 2011

'HAS HE DELIBERATELY CHOSEN A LEAGUE I AM NOT INVOLVED IN?'

*On Pep Guardiola being announced as the
new manager of Bayern Munich, 2013*

JOSÉ ON
PLAYERS

'HOW DO YOU SAY CHEATING IN CATALAN?'

On Lionel Messi's involvement in Asier del Horno getting sent off during a Champions League match between Chelsea and Barcelona, 2006

**'CAN MESSI BE
SUSPENDED FOR
ACTING? BARCELONA IS
A CULTURAL CITY WITH
MANY GREAT THEATRES
AND THIS BOY HAS
LEARNED VERY WELL'**

On Lionel Messi, 2006

'RONALDO IS A GOOD
PLAYER, BUT HE IS
CERTAINLY NOT THE
BEST. HE DESERVED THE
GOLDEN BALL BECAUSE
HIS TEAM WON THE
CHAMPIONS LEAGUE
AND THE PREMIER
LEAGUE'

*On his Inter striker Zlatan Ibrahimovic
not winning the Ballon d'Or, 2008*

'PEPE'S COMMENTS? IT IS VERY EASY TO ANALYSE WHAT HE SAYS. PEPE HAS A PROBLEM AND HIS NAME IS RAPHAEL VARANE. A 31-YEAR-OLD HAS LOST HIS PLACE TO A 19-YEAR-OLD. IT'S THE LAW OF LIFE'

On criticisms from dropped Real Madrid defender Pepe, 2013

'RICARDO CARVALHO SEEMS TO HAVE PROBLEMS UNDERSTANDING THINGS, MAYBE HE SHOULD HAVE AN IQ TEST, OR GO TO A MENTAL HOSPITAL'

On defender Carvalho's complaints after being dropped, 2005

'AS YOU KNOW GALLAS HAD AN UNBELIEVABLE HOLIDAY. I HOPE HE ENJOYED IT VERY MUCH IN GUADELOUPE, WHICH I THINK IS A FANTASTIC PLACE'

On defender William Gallas failing to turn up for Chelsea's pre-season tour to the US, 2006

'TELL DECO I'M PISSED OFF – I WANT MORE'

*Text message to Porto bench during
UEFA Cup semi-final when Mourinho
was banished to the stands, 2003*

'I WENT THERE AND I WAS THINKING IF THEY WANT TO PUT HIM ON THE DARK SIDE I HAVE TO PUSH HIM UP. IF THEY WANT TO PUT HIM ON THE MOON, I HAVE TO PRAISE HIM. SO BECAUSE HE GOT ALL THE PLAUDITS FROM THE PRESS, I HAD TO KICK HIM A LITTLE BIT'

On man-managing Joe Cole, 2004

'MAKELELE IS NOT A FOOTBALL PLAYER – MAKELELE IS A SLAVE'

On French coach Raymond Domenech picking Claude Makelele for a European Championship qualifier, despite Makelele having retired from international football, 2006

'IT WILL BE A BIG TEST.
FOR THEM'

*On Barcelona's Ronaldinho and Samuel Eto'o,
facing a then up-and-coming John Terry, 2005*

JOSÉ VERSUS LIVERPOOL

'LIVERPOOL ARE NOT A BIG TEAM. TO HAVE NOT WON THE LEAGUE FOR ALMOST 15 YEARS IS NOT GOOD ENOUGH'

After losing to Liverpool in the 2006 FA Cup semi-final

'IT WAS A GOAL THAT CAME FROM THE MOON, FROM THE ANFIELD STANDS... LIVERPOOL SCORED IF YOU CAN SAY THAT THEY SCORED, BECAUSE MAYBE YOU SHOULD SAY THE LINESMAN SCORED'

On losing to Liverpool in the 2005 Champions League

'THEIR FANS CAN CONTINUE TO CHANT "NO HISTORY" AT US BUT WE CONTINUE TO MAKE IT'

On chants from Liverpool supporters, 2007

'THE BEST TEAM LOST. AFTER THEY SCORED ONLY ONE TEAM PLAYED, THE OTHER ONE JUST DEFENDED FOR THE WHOLE GAME'

On losing to Liverpool in the Champions League semi-final, 2005

'IF YOU'RE NOT A BIG CLUB, YOU CHOOSE ONE COMPETITION AND FIGHT IN THAT COMPETITION AND FORGET THE OTHERS. BIG CLUBS – WE CANNOT DO THIS'

On Liverpool, prior to Chelsea's Champions League semi-final against them, 2007

'TWO FINALS IN THREE YEARS – NOT BAD FOR A LITTLE CLUB'

Steven Gerrard on Liverpool knocking out Chelsea to reach the Champions League final, 2007

ARSENE AND
SIR ALEX

'I UNDERSTAND WHY HE
IS A BIT EMOTIONAL. HE
HAS SOME OF THE TOP
PLAYERS IN THE WORLD
AND THEY SHOULD BE
DOING A LOT BETTER
THAN THAT'

*On Sir Alex Ferguson's response to
Porto knocking Manchester United
out of the Champions League, 2004…*

'YOU WOULD BE SAD IF YOUR TEAM GETS AS CLEARLY DOMINATED BY OPPONENTS WHO HAVE BEEN BUILT ON 10% OF THE BUDGET'

… and not remotely rubbing salt into the wounds

'I THINK HE IS ONE OF
THOSE PEOPLE WHO IS
A VOYEUR. HE LIKES TO
WATCH OTHER PEOPLE.
THERE ARE SOME GUYS
WHO, WHEN THEY
ARE AT HOME, HAVE
A BIG TELESCOPE TO
SEE WHAT HAPPENS IN
OTHER FAMILIES'

On Arsene Wenger, 2005

'OUT OF ORDER, DISCONNECTED WITH REALITY AND DISRESPECTFUL'

Arsene Wenger on Mourinho's 'voyeur' comments, 2005

'I SAW THEIR PLAYERS AND MANAGER GO FOR A LAP OF HONOUR AFTER LOSING TO US IN THEIR LAST HOME GAME. IN PORTUGAL IF YOU DO THIS, THEY THROW BOTTLES AT YOU'

*On Manchester United's lap of 'honour',
having been beaten by Chelsea in their
last home game of the season, 2005*

'HE IS A SPECIALIST
ON FAILURE. I'M NOT.
THE REALITY IS, HE IS
A SPECIALIST. EIGHT
YEARS WITHOUT A
PIECE OF SILVERWARE,
THAT'S FAILURE'

On Arsene Wenger, 2014

'MAYBE WHEN I TURN 60 AND HAVE BEEN MANAGING IN THE SAME LEAGUE FOR 20 YEARS AND HAVE THE RESPECT OF EVERYBODY, I WILL HAVE THE POWER TO SPEAK TO PEOPLE AND MAKE THEM TREMBLE A BIT'

On Sir Alex Ferguson, 2005

'AFTER THE GAME
ON WEDNESDAY WE
WERE TOGETHER IN MY
OFFICE AND WE SPOKE
AND DRANK WINE.
UNFORTUNATELY, IT WAS
A VERY BAD BOTTLE
OF WINE AND HE WAS
COMPLAINING'

On a post-match drink with Sir Alex, 2005

'IF THEY DON'T TOUCH ME, I WON'T TOUCH ANYONE. IF THEY TOUCH ME, I'LL BE READY TO HIT BACK EVEN HARDER'

A warning to Alex Ferguson and Arsene Wenger, 2004

RAFA AND RANIERI

'I DON'T WANT TO WIN THE EUROPA LEAGUE. IT WOULD BE A BIG DISAPPOINTMENT FOR ME'

On Rafa Benitez leading Chelsea to the trophy in 2013

'I THOUGHT HE WAS GOING TO THANK ME FOR THE TITLE I GAVE HIM. INTER FANS WOULD TELL YOU HOW THEY REALLY FEEL ABOUT IT'

Mourinho congratulates Rafa Benitez on winning the Club World Cup with Inter Milan, 2010

'I STUDIED ITALIAN FIVE HOURS A DAY FOR MANY MONTHS TO ENSURE I COULD COMMUNICATE WITH THE PLAYERS, THE MEDIA, THE FANS. RANIERI HAD BEEN IN ENGLAND FOR FIVE YEARS AND STILL STRUGGLED TO SAY "GOOD MORNING"'

On his Chelsea predecessor and then Juventus manager Claudio Ranieri, 2008

'HE HAS WON A SUPER CUP, A SMALL CUP. HE HAS NEVER WON A MAJOR TROPHY. MAYBE HE NEEDS TO CHANGE HIS MINDSET BUT HE IS TOO OLD TO DO IT'

On Ranieri's managerial achievements, 2008

'BOREDOM BY RANIERI? IS IT LIKE SARTRE'S *NAUSEA*, WHICH I USED TO STUDY?'

Responding to criticisms by Claudio Ranieri
of his Inter side being dull to watch, 2008

'IF I DID THAT THEY'D JUST LAUGH AT ME AND THINK I WAS SICK'

*On Claudio Ranieri's motivational
methods of making his players
watch the film* Gladiator, *2004*

'THREE YEARS WITHOUT A PREMIERSHIP TITLE? I DON'T THINK I WOULD STILL BE IN A JOB'

On then Liverpool manager Rafa Benitez, 2007

'I THINK I HAVE A NAÏVE TEAM. THEY ARE NAÏVE BECAUSE THEY ARE PURE AND CLEAN. WE DON'T HAVE DIVERS'

On a contentious penalty won by Florent Malouda against Liverpool, 2007

'IF CHELSEA ARE NAÏVE AND PURE, THEN I'M LITTLE RED RIDING HOOD'

Benitez not quite buying the argument, 2007

'ME AND JOSÉ WERE REALLY GOOD FRIENDS UNTIL LIVERPOOL STARTED BEATING THEM'

Rafa Benitez on José Mourinho, 2009

JOSÉ IN ITALY

'THE PRESIDENT GAVE ME A BEAUTIFUL BOOK ABOUT INTER'S HISTORY, BUT WE NEED TO WRITE A NEW BOOK'

On taking over at Inter, 2008

'I COULD HAVE PLAYED IN GOAL AND WE WOULD STILL HAVE WON'

On Inter Milan's 2-1 win over Catania, 2008

'I DO NOT KNOW WHO HE IS. I HAVE HEARD OF BAYERN MONACO AND THE MONACO GP, THE TIBETAN MONACO AND THE PRINCIPALITY OF MONACO. I'VE NEVER HEARD OF ANY OTHERS'

On incensed Catania director Pietro Lo Monaco, who claimed Mourinho deserved 'a smack in the mouth', 2008

'ZEMAN? I DO NOT KNOW HIM. WHERE DOES HE PLAY? IS HE A COACH? SORRY, I DID NOT KNOW THAT. NOW THAT I AM ON HOLIDAY I WILL LOOK HIM UP ON GOOGLE TO FIND OUT WHO HE IS AND WHAT HE HAS WON'

On Roma coach Zdenek Zeman, who described Mourinho as a 'mediocre coach', 2012

'WE WOULD HAVE WON THIS GAME EVEN WITH SEVEN MEN. MAYBE WITH SIX WE WOULD HAVE STRUGGLED, BUT WE WOULD HAVE WON WITH SEVEN'

*On Inter being reduced to nine men but
still beating AC Milan 2-0, 2010*

'I DON'T STICK MY HEAD IN THE SAND, I KNOW THERE IS ONLY ONE TEAM THAT HAS A PENALTY AREA 25 METRES LONG'

*On the supposed referee bias
towards Juventus, 2010*

'EVERYTHING WAS DONE TODAY TO TRY AND PREVENT INTER FROM WINNING, BUT MY SQUAD IS STRONG AND WE WILL WIN THE SCUDETTO. BUT I WILL LEAVE IT AT THAT. THIS IS YOUR COUNTRY AND YOUR LEAGUE. I AM JUST A FOREIGNER WORKING HERE'

On Inter, 2010

'I AM VERY HAPPY AT INTER. I AM NOT HAPPY IN ITALIAN FOOTBALL – BECAUSE I DON'T LIKE IT AND THEY DON'T LIKE ME. SIMPLE'

On life in Italy, 2010

'ZERU TITULI'

Mourinho claims that Inter's rivals would finish the season with 'no titles'. His mispronunciation (it should have been zero titoli) ended up being used on T-shirts by Inter fans

'PEOPLE WERE WILLING TO KILL FOR HIM'

Zlatan Ibrahimovic on his then Inter boss, 2013

'WHAT AM I TO DO? RETIRE? AFTER YOU, I CAN'T HAVE ANOTHER COACH'

Inter defender Materazzi on the news that Mourinho is leaving, 2010

JOSÉ ON
MANAGEMENT

'FOR ME, PRESSURE
IS BIRD FLU'

*On successfully defending Chelsea's Premier
League title (concerns about a bird flu epidemic
were in the news at the time)*

'WHEN I GO TO A PRESS CONFERENCE BEFORE THE GAME, IN MY MIND THE GAME HAS ALREADY STARTED'

Interview with World Soccer, *2004*

'IF HE HELPED ME OUT IN TRAINING WE WOULD BE BOTTOM OF THE LEAGUE AND IF I HAD TO WORK IN HIS WORLD OF BIG BUSINESS, WE WOULD BE BANKRUPT'

On Roman Abramovich, 2005

'WHAT PRESSURE? PRESSURE IS POOR PEOPLE IN THE WORLD TRYING TO FEED THEIR FAMILIES. THERE IS NO PRESSURE IN FOOTBALL'

Keeping his cool after losing to Barcelona and Blackburn, 2005

'FEAR IS NOT A WORD IN MY FOOTBALL DICTIONARY'

Some linguistic thoughts, 2010

'I WOULD RATHER PLAY WITH 10 MEN THAN WAIT FOR A PLAYER WHO IS LATE FOR THE BUS'

On discipline, 2011

'AFTER 15 YEARS, I'M AN OVERNIGHT SUCCESS'

On making it as a manager, 2004

'HE HAS TO BE A LEADER OF MEN AND A COHERENT LEADER. HE MUST MAKE ALL HIS MEN FEEL BIG, NOT SMALL'

On being a manager, 2005

JOSÉ IN SPAIN

'I WOULD ONLY EVER COACH REAL MADRID TO DESTROY THEM: I WILL NEVER STOP BEING A CULÉ*'

On leaving Barcelona, but Barcelona not leaving him, 2000

(*Culé is a nickname for Barça fans. It means 'bottom' and comes from the fact that in the 1920s at their old stadium, fans would sit on the top of a wall to watch them, so all anyone could see from the outside was a row of backsides)

'I DAMAGED SPANISH FOOTBALL BY BEING THE MANAGER THAT BROKE BARCELONA DOMINANCE'

On Andres Iniesta's suggestion that he had 'damaged' Spanish football, 2013

'I AM ALWAYS HOPING THERE IS SOME "SMART GUY" WHO WILL ASK ME A QUESTION WHICH REQUIRES A PIECE OF PAPER'

Responding positively to a question at a Real Madrid press conference, 2013

'MY WORK IS NEVER VALUED IN ABSOLUTE TERMS BUT IN TERMS OF WHAT I HAVE ACHIEVED AND THAT'S MY FAULT BECAUSE I HAVE WON SO MUCH'

On why the press give him a hard time, 2013

'YOU JOURNALISTS WILL WANT TO WIPE ME OFF THE LIST BUT YOU WON'T BE ABLE TO... THE RECORD [IS] MINE, IT CAN'T BE DELETED'

Reminding a critical Spanish press of Real Madrid's record-breaking 2011–12 season, when they won La Liga with 100 points and scored 121 goals

'YOU ARE TRAITORS...
YOU ARE THE MOST
TREACHEROUS SQUAD
I'VE HAD IN MY LIFE'

*On discovering that someone leaked his tactics
prior to Real Madrid facing Barcelona, 2011*

'I'M NOT BOTHERED BY THE WHISTLES AT ME. IT'S NOT A PROBLEM'

On being booed by Real Madrid fans, 2012

'CANELLA... HE'S A VERY BAD COLLEAGUE, AN OUT-OF-CONTROL EGOMANIAC... I'D LIKE TO PUT HIM UP IN THE STANDS FOR AN EVENING WITH OUR ULTRA BOYS'

*Manolo Preciado of Sporting Gijón, on Mourinho's claim his team had eased up in a match against Barcelona (*canella *means 'low-life')*

'INACCESSIBLE, DISRESPECTFUL AND WITHOUT A MINIMUM SENSE OF DIGNITY'

Valencia manager Unai Emery responds to Mourinho accusing him of being 'fragile'

HEY, GOOD-LOOKING

'BRING YOUR SISTER ALONG AND WE CAN FIND OUT IF THAT'S TRUE'

After being asked by journalist Santi Jimenez if he was Sir Bobby Robson's boyfriend, 1996

'I LIKE THE LOOK OF MOURINHO. THERE'S A BIT OF THE YOUNG CLOUGH TO HIM. FOR A START, HE'S GOOD-LOOKING...'

Brian Clough on Mourinho, 2004

'I THINK THEY SHOULD GET GEORGE CLOONEY TO PLAY ME. HE'S A FANTASTIC ACTOR AND MY WIFE THINKS HE WOULD BE IDEAL'

On who should get the starring role in a film of his life, 2004

'LOOK AT MY HAIRCUT. I AM READY FOR THE WAR'

On his new haircut, 2006

'YOUR COAT'S FROM
MATALAN...'

Terrace chant from rival fans to José's
favourite choice of attire, 2005

'MY WIFE WILL BE
GLAD ABOUT MOURINHO
COMING TO BRAMALL
LANE BECAUSE HE'S
A GOOD-LOOKING
SWINE, ISN'T HE?'

*Then Sheffield United manager
Neil Warnock, 2006*

JOSÉ VERSUS
THE WORLD

'I DON'T SHAKE HANDS WITH PEOPLE I DON'T KNOW'

On why he wouldn't shake hands with Boavista manager Jaime Pacheco, 2003

'PRESSURE ON THE LINESMAN, EVERYBODY!'

Text message sent from Mourinho to the dug-out, during his suspension at the 2003 UEFA Cup semi-final

'SECOND PLACE IS JUST
THE FIRST LOSER. IF
MADRID WERE TO FIRE
ME, I WOULDN'T GO
TO MALAGA. I'D GO TO
A TOP-LEVEL TEAM IN
ITALY OR ENGLAND'

*On Manuel Pellegrini, his predecessor
as Real Madrid manager, 2010*

'HE MADE A FIVE-A-SIDE TEAM BECAUSE I PLAYED WITH ONLY FIVE PLAYERS FROM HIS TEAM'

On Roberto Mancini's claim that
Mourinho inherited a great team
when he replaced him at Inter, 2014

'[AN] ENEMY
OF FOOTBALL'

*UEFA Referees Committee Chairman
Volker Roth on Mourinho after comments
about Anders Frisk, 2005*

'MR ROTH HAS TWO WAYS OUT, APOLOGISE OR IT GOES TO COURT'

Mourinho in response. He never received an apology, but did not sue Roth, 2005

'I DON'T WANT HIM TO TEACH ME HOW TO LOSE 4-0 IN A CHAMPIONS LEAGUE FINAL BECAUSE I DON'T WANT TO LEARN THAT'

On criticisms from Johan Cruyff about his tactics, 2005 (Cruyff was manager at Barcelona when they lost 4-0 to AC Milan in the 1994 final)

MRS MOURINHO

'IT ALL DEPENDS ON MY WIFE. IF I AM HOME, YES, I WILL SEE IT... BUT MAYBE I WILL HAVE NO PERMISSION'

On whether he will be watching the Manchester United-Arsenal clash, 2004

'MY WIFE IS IN PORTUGAL WITH THE DOG. THE DOG IS WITH MY WIFE SO THE CITY OF LONDON IS SAFE'

On being questioned by the police over his lack of a 'pet passport' for his Yorkshire Terrier, 2007

'I'M NOT EVEN THE BOSS AT HOME – THAT'S MY WIFE!'

On life in the Mourinho household, 2012

'WHAT POSITION IS MY WIFE IN? EIGHTH AT LEAST'

On being placed ninth in a poll of the most influential men in the world

JOSÉ ON JOSÉ

'I AM NOT WORRIED ABOUT PRESSURE. IF I WANTED TO HAVE AN EASY JOB I WOULD HAVE STAYED AT PORTO. BEAUTIFUL BLUE CHAIR, THE UEFA CHAMPIONS LEAGUE TROPHY, GOD, AND AFTER GOD, ME'

On taking the Chelsea job, 2004

'WE HAVE TOP PLAYERS AND, SORRY IF I'M ARROGANT, A TOP MANAGER'

On arriving at Chelsea, 2004

'AT THAT TIME, I WAS
SAYING I WAS SPECIAL
BECAUSE I WAS
EUROPEAN CHAMPION
TWO DAYS BEFORE THAT
SO I ARRIVED HERE WITH
MY EGO THIS BIG. NOW,
IT'S EVEN HIGHER!'

*Looking back at the 'Special One'
press conference a year later*

'WHY HAVE CHELSEA SUFFERED SO MUCH SINCE I LEFT? BECAUSE I LEFT'

On Chelsea's post-Mourinho struggles, 2009

'JUST IMAGINE IF I DID – I WOULD DIE IN THE CRUSH OUT IN THE MIDDLE OF THE PITCH'

Citing safety reasons for not returning to say goodbye to Chelsea fans after leaving, 2007

'I DON'T LIKE TO SAY THAT I'M A MAN WITH TWO FACES, BUT JOSÉ MOURINHO THE MANAGER AND THE MAN ARE VERY DIFFERENT. IT'S IMPORTANT TO SEPARATE THEM AND I DO THAT VERY EASILY'

On being Mourinho, 2005

'HE MUST THINK I'M A GREAT GUY. HE MUST THINK THAT, BECAUSE OTHERWISE HE WOULD NOT HAVE GIVEN ME SO MUCH... HE MUST HAVE A VERY HIGH OPINION OF ME.'

On God, 2011